MAYER SMITH

Embers Beneath the Silver Sky

Copyright © 2025 by Mayer Smith

All rights reserved. No part of this publication may be reproduced, stored or transmitted in any form or by any means, electronic, mechanical, photocopying, recording, scanning, or otherwise without written permission from the publisher. It is illegal to copy this book, post it to a website, or distribute it by any other means without permission.

This novel is entirely a work of fiction. The names, characters and incidents portrayed in it are the work of the author's imagination. Any resemblance to actual persons, living or dead, events or localities is entirely coincidental.

Mayer Smith asserts the moral right to be identified as the author of this work.

Mayer Smith has no responsibility for the persistence or accuracy of URLs for external or third-party Internet Websites referred to in this publication and does not guarantee that any content on such Websites is, or will remain, accurate or appropriate.

Designations used by companies to distinguish their products are often claimed as trademarks. All brand names and product names used in this book and on its cover are trade names, service marks, trademarks and registered trademarks of their respective owners. The publishers and the book are not associated with any product or vendor mentioned in this book. None of the companies referenced within the book have endorsed the book.

First edition

This book was professionally typeset on Reedsy. Find out more at reedsy.com

Contents

1	The Ashes of Yesterday	1
2	Shadows in the Smoke	7
3	Whispers of a Forgotten Wind	15
4	The Ruins of Fire and Sky	24
5	A Debt to the Dark	31
6	Hearts Against the Storm	39
7	The Betrayer's Embrace	46
8	The Silver Sky Fractures	53
9	The Fire Within	60
10	Love and Ruin	67
11	The Final Ember	73
12	The Silver Sky	79

One

The Ashes of Yesterday

The world smelled of dying embers.

Kael stood at the edge of the market square, his hand resting lightly on the hilt of his sword, watching the way the night twisted with secrets. Firelight flickered against stone walls, casting wavering shadows that moved like phantoms. The scent of roasted meat and damp earth mingled with something fainter—blood, just beginning to cool.

The oracle lay sprawled in the dust.

Her frail body was twisted, silver hair spilling across the ground like molten moonlight. A thin dagger jutted from her side, the hilt marked with an unfamiliar insignia. Kael exhaled sharply. The city of Ravoss was no stranger to death, but this was different. This was meant to send a message.

And yet, the old woman still clung to life.

Her fingers trembled as she reached for him, her breath rattling in her chest. "The Silver Sky," she whispered. "It will break when fire and air become one."

Kael stiffened. He knelt beside her, careful, wary. "What does that mean?"

The oracle's lips parted, but no answer came. Only a sigh. A flicker of something in her gaze—recognition, or perhaps warning. Then, she was gone, her body settling into stillness, leaving behind only the weight of her final words.

A low murmur rippled through the gathered onlookers, fear rising like a slow tide.

Kael didn't have time for prophecy or riddles. He had spent too many years chasing ghosts, only to find them leading him in circles. What mattered now was the dagger. A weapon like that didn't belong to street thieves or common mercenaries.

Someone had killed her with purpose.

A shiver skated down his spine. He had spent years hunting men who killed with precision, and this—this was the work of someone who knew exactly what they were doing.

The crowd began to shift, uneasy, but Kael felt it before he saw it—the presence in the shadows, a figure slipping away into the alley beyond the square.

He moved.

The night pressed against his skin as he followed, his boots silent against the uneven stone. The city was a labyrinth at this hour, its twisting alleys steeped in a hush that only deepened the sense of danger. Whoever he was chasing had the advantage.

Kael didn't stop.

He rounded a corner just in time to see a cloaked figure vault onto a low rooftop, their movement fluid, practiced. His muscles tensed. Whoever they were, they were fast. Trained. Dangerous.

But so was he.

He pushed forward, grabbing onto the worn edge of the stone wall and hauling himself up. The figure was already moving, leaping across the rooftops, and Kael followed, the chase narrowing the world into nothing but the rhythmic pounding of his feet against the tiles and the sharp pull of night air in his lungs.

Then—an opening. A misstep.

The cloaked figure faltered, just for a heartbeat, but it was enough.

Kael lunged, grabbing hold of the fabric, yanking them backward. They twisted, striking out, but he caught their wrist, forcing them down. The hood fell back, and the sight beneath it made his breath hitch.

A woman.

And not just any woman.

Her hair was dark as the night sky, long strands slipping loose from their bindings. Her eyes were a storm waiting to break—grey, sharp, filled with something too close to defiance. A delicate scar curved along her temple, half-hidden beneath the loose strands of her hair.

For a moment, neither of them moved.

The tension stretched between them, crackling, alive.

Then, with a sudden twist, she broke free.

Kael swore, blocking the strike she aimed at his ribs, barely dodging the blade she pulled from her belt. She was faster than he had expected, her movements precise, but there was something else beneath her skill—something desperate.

She wasn't just running. She was running from something.

"Who sent you?" he demanded.

The woman didn't answer. Instead, she feinted left before pivoting sharply, her heel slamming into his ribs. The force sent him stumbling, and by the time he righted himself, she was already leaping to the next rooftop.

The Ashes of Yesterday

Kael took a breath, steadying himself.

He had her scent now.

She wouldn't disappear so easily.

Elsewhere in the City

Selene pressed herself against the cold stone wall of a narrow alley, her pulse hammering. The fire-wielder had almost caught her.

He moved like a warrior, but there was something else in the way he fought—something relentless. He wasn't just a hired blade. He had training. Control.

And she had seen the way his eyes locked onto hers.

Recognition.

She exhaled slowly, flexing her fingers. The air around her stirred, the faintest whisper of wind responding to her—but no more than that. Magic was dead. It had been for years.

Except... if the oracle's words were true, that was about to change.

A tremor passed through her. She had never believed in fate, but she had spent too long running from ghosts to ignore them now. The Silver Sky will break. Fire and air.

Her lips pressed together.

Kael.

She had heard his name spoken before, though always in whispers. A warrior once bound to a kingdom that no longer existed. A man who had walked through fire and come out burned but unbroken.

And now, he was hunting her.

Selene drew in a breath, forcing herself to move. If she stayed here too long, others would find her. The same people who had sent that dagger into the oracle's side wouldn't hesitate to do the same to her.

She turned, slipping into the shadows.

She had to find the ruins before he found her.

Because if the prophecy was true, if magic was truly returning…

Then Kael wasn't just a threat.

He was the only person in the world who could destroy her—or save her.

And she had no idea which.

Two

Shadows in the Smoke

The scent of charred wood clung to Kael's skin, the dying embers of Ravoss casting a dull orange glow against the streets. Somewhere in the distance, a bell tolled—a somber sound, warning of another death. The city was shifting beneath him, thick with whispers, but his focus remained on one thing.

The woman.

Selene.

He had spent years learning the difference between those who ran and those who hunted while running. She was the latter. Her movements, her eyes, the way she fought—she wasn't just another fugitive. She knew things. Things that could either get her killed or change the fate of something much larger.

And now, she was gone.

Kael exhaled, adjusting the strap of the sword across his back as he moved through the market district, scanning the alleys, the rooftops, anywhere she might have disappeared. Ravoss was a city of shifting loyalties, where gold mattered more than honor. It wouldn't be long before someone else caught her scent.

Which meant he had to find her first.

The silver-feathered dagger still weighed heavily in his grip. It wasn't just an assassin's tool—it was a mark. A signature. And the last time Kael had seen one, it had been buried in the chest of a dying nobleman.

The Silver Order.

He clenched his jaw. He hadn't heard their name in years, but if they were involved… then whatever Selene was running from, it wasn't just mercenaries or common bounty hunters. It was something much worse.

A shift in the wind made him pause. The air was changing, carrying something with it—something familiar. The faintest trace of warmth against the night's chill.

Not fire.

Not entirely.

Magic.

Kael turned sharply, his gaze narrowing on a figure moving through the smoke-filled streets, barely visible beneath the heavy hood she wore. But it was her. He didn't need to see her face to know.

Selene.

She was moving quickly, slipping between the thinning crowd, her steps precise, measured. She didn't know he had found her.

Not yet.

Kael stepped forward, matching her pace. Not chasing this time—stalking.

He had questions.

And she was going to answer them.

Selene felt the shift before she saw him.
The air around her pressed in, as if sensing something closing in behind her. The weight of a stare, the tension of a predator watching his prey.

She knew better than to run.

Instead, she slowed. Just enough to let him make his move.

And he did.

A hand closed around her wrist, firm but controlled. The

warmth of his skin was unexpected—fire lingered there, even in his touch. She didn't fight. Not yet.

"Running again?" Kael's voice was quiet, edged with something unreadable.

Selene turned her head just enough to meet his gaze. Those dark amber eyes studied her, searching, calculating. There was no malice in them, but there was something worse.

Curiosity.

That could be dangerous.

"I prefer the term surviving," she said smoothly, her voice barely above a whisper.

Kael's grip didn't loosen.

"You were at the oracle's side when she died," he said. "You knew her."

Selene didn't answer.

He stepped closer. "And now you're running. That tells me something."

Selene tilted her head slightly, her lips curving into the barest hint of a smile. "Does it?"

His jaw tightened, his patience thinning. "You don't strike me as a fool," he said. "So I'm going to assume you already know the kind of people who are after you."

Selene met his gaze fully now. "And I assume you already know the kind of people who are after you," she countered. "Tell me, Kael—why does the Silver Order have an interest in you?"

His expression flickered, just for a fraction of a second. It was enough.

Selene had spent her life learning how to read people, and Kael wasn't as unreadable as he thought.

He was just good at hiding what haunted him.

She took advantage of his momentary silence, slipping free from his grasp. Kael let her, but he didn't move away.

"Why did the oracle say what she did?" he asked. "What does the Silver Sky have to do with you?"

Selene hesitated.

She could lie. She could run.

But something about the way he looked at her—like he wasn't just demanding answers, but trying to understand something—made her pause.

Maybe because the same questions haunted her, too.

She inhaled, turning fully toward him. "Magic is not dead," she said quietly. "Not yet."

Kael didn't react at first. Then, he tilted his head slightly, studying her. "What do you mean?"

Selene glanced around, wary of listening ears. "Not here," she murmured. "There's an abandoned temple on the outskirts. If you want answers, meet me there."

Kael's gaze flickered, assessing the offer.

She expected him to hesitate.

Instead, he gave a slow nod. "I'll be there."

Selene turned, slipping back into the shadows.

She didn't trust him.

But she wasn't sure she could afford not to.

The Ruins of Fire and Sky

The temple had been abandoned for years, swallowed by time and neglect. Vines coiled around its broken pillars, and the scent of damp stone filled the air.

Selene stood beneath its crumbling archway, waiting.

She didn't have to wait long.

Shadows in the Smoke

Footsteps echoed through the silence.

Kael emerged from the darkness, moving with the quiet confidence of a man who had spent years walking battlefields.

He stopped a few paces from her. "You made it," she said, her voice lighter than she felt.

Kael folded his arms. "You have answers."

Selene exhaled. "Not enough."

She moved toward the temple's altar, brushing dust from its surface. "The world thinks magic is gone. But magic doesn't disappear. It fades. It lingers. It waits."

Kael watched her, silent.

She placed a hand on the altar's cold stone. "The Silver Sky will break when fire and air become one," she murmured. "I don't know what it means. But I know I'm not the only one searching for the answer."

She turned to face him. "And neither are you."

The firelight flickered across Kael's face, casting shadows in the hollows of his expression. "You think magic can come back," he said. Not a question. A statement.

Selene hesitated. Then, softly—

"I think it never truly left."

The wind stirred, whispering through the ruins. Kael studied her for a long moment, unreadable.

Then, finally, he nodded.

"We find the answers," he said. "Together."

Selene's breath caught, just for a second.

She hadn't meant to let him in.

But maybe, just maybe—

She needed him, too.

And that thought was more dangerous than all the enemies waiting in the dark.

Three

Whispers of a Forgotten Wind

T he ruins held their breath.

Selene stood motionless beneath the fractured archway, her fingers pressed lightly against the altar's worn stone. The temple had been abandoned for decades, yet it still hummed with something just beneath the surface—something old, something waiting.

Kael leaned against a broken column a few paces away, watching her with the quiet intensity of a man used to seeing danger in the shadows. His presence filled the space in a way that unsettled her more than it should. He was still, but not at ease—coiled like a blade yet to be unsheathed.

She exhaled slowly, willing the tension from her muscles.

"This place," she murmured. "It used to be sacred."

Kael's voice was steady, unreadable. "To whom?"

Selene let her hand trace the outline of the ancient carvings embedded in the stone. Symbols of air, fire, and the celestial forces that had once bound the world. "The Keepers of Balance," she said. "A sect devoted to preserving the ties between magic and the elements."

Kael's silence was its own question.

She turned to face him fully. "Before magic faded, it was believed that fire and air were the closest of all the elements. One feeds the other. But they can also destroy each other."

His amber eyes flickered, the firelight from the lone brazier casting shadows across his sharp features. "You're saying the prophecy isn't just about restoring magic," he said. "It's about a choice."

Selene studied him carefully. He understood things too quickly, too keenly. He wasn't just a warrior. He was something else—something dangerous.

And yet, she hadn't told him to leave.

Not yet.

A gust of wind pushed through the broken temple, lifting the strands of her hair.

Whispers of a Forgotten Wind

Selene stilled.

For a heartbeat, she felt it.

Not just the wind's presence—but its intent.

It curled around her like an old friend, whispering against her skin, urging, urging—

Then it was gone.

The absence was so sudden it left her breathless.

Her hand clenched at her side, fingers curling into a fist. She had been right. Magic hadn't disappeared—it was hiding, buried beneath the bones of the world, waiting to be awakened.

She turned back to Kael, choosing her words carefully.

"There's something happening, Kael. The wind…" She hesitated, uncertain if she should reveal just how much she felt. "It's not dead."

He didn't laugh. Didn't scoff. He only watched her, his expression unreadable. "And fire?"

Selene's breath hitched, but she masked it quickly.

Fire and air.

One could not exist without the other.

She had spent her entire life believing she would never again wield the winds. That the elements had abandoned her. And yet, here was Kael, a man who carried fire in his blood, standing before her like some cruel twist of fate.

The prophecy's words echoed in her mind.

The Silver Sky will break when fire and air become one.

Selene swallowed. "If fire is still alive…" She met his gaze, her voice barely above a whisper. "Then so is the storm."

Kael straightened slightly, sensing the shift in her tone. "What do you mean?"

Selene hesitated. Then she turned back toward the altar. "Come here."

He didn't move immediately. But then, slowly, he stepped forward, stopping just beside her. She could feel the heat radiating from him—something that had nothing to do with the cool night air.

Selene pressed a palm to the stone and motioned for him to do the same.

Kael hesitated. His fingers flexed slightly before he placed his hand beside hers.

For a moment, nothing happened.

Then the air changed.

The temperature rose, the faintest whisper of warmth curling beneath Selene's palm. The ruins trembled—just a fraction, as if something unseen had stirred beneath them.

Selene's pulse pounded.

It wasn't much.

But it was enough.

She turned her gaze upward, to the sky above them, where the stars flickered like dying embers.

Something was coming.

And they had just awakened it.

Kael felt it, too.
 A pulse of warmth. A shift in the air.

The sensation burned through his veins, unsettling and familiar all at once.

He pulled his hand back, flexing his fingers. "What did we just do?"

Selene's eyes remained fixed on the sky. "The balance is shifting," she murmured. "Someone has been trying to keep it from breaking." She exhaled, her breath slow and deliberate.

"But we just fractured it."

Kael tensed. "Meaning?"

Her gaze flickered to him, and for the first time, there was something almost like fear in her expression. "Meaning they'll come for us now."

The words sent an old, familiar chill down his spine.

It had been years since he had felt that kind of certainty—that moment before a war began.

Kael let out a slow breath. "Then we need to leave."

Selene nodded, but before they could move, something shifted in the ruins. A rustling. A whisper of movement.

Kael's instincts flared to life.

He turned sharply—just in time to see a figure emerging from the shadows.

A masked man. Cloaked in grey, the silver insignia of a feather glinting against the moonlight.

Selene froze.

Kael's grip tightened on his sword.

The man spoke, his voice smooth, unhurried. "You shouldn't

have come here."

Kael stepped slightly in front of Selene. "I was just about to say the same thing."

The masked man tilted his head, as if amused. "Do you have any idea what you've done?"

Selene swallowed, her voice careful. "The balance was already shifting," she said. "We didn't break it."

The man let out a soft chuckle. "You misunderstand."

Kael's pulse hammered. He didn't like the way this man spoke—calm, collected, as if he already knew how this would end.

And then—

The wind shifted.

It wasn't like before.

It was sharp. Cold.

And filled with a voice that did not belong to the living.

Kael barely had time to react before the shadows in the ruins began to move.

Selene gasped, her breath hitching as tendrils of darkness slithered toward them, wrapping around the stones like serpents.

The masked man stepped back, his figure blurring—

Then he was gone.

A whisper of wind rushed past Kael's ear.

"Find the ember before the storm takes it."

And then—

The ruins collapsed.

Kael grabbed Selene's wrist and ran.

The ground cracked beneath their feet, stone crumbling as something ancient and unseen rose from the depths. Dust and debris filled the air, choking the night with the scent of burning magic.

They barely made it past the archway before the ruins imploded, sinking into themselves with a final, deafening roar.

Silence followed.

Kael exhaled, releasing Selene's wrist.

She was staring at the destruction, her expression unreadable.

Kael took a step closer. "Tell me," he said, his voice quiet but firm. "What the hell just happened?"

Selene didn't look at him.

Her gaze lifted toward the sky, where the first wisps of silver clouds had begun to gather.

"The storm," she whispered.

"It's coming."

Four

The Ruins of Fire and Sky

The wind had changed. It wasn't just the shift in the air, or the way the ground trembled beneath their feet. It was something deeper. Something that vibrated in Kael's chest, like the first stirrings of an oncoming storm.

Selene stood a few paces away from him, her silhouette outlined against the dying light of the temple ruins. Her eyes were fixed on the horizon, where dark clouds had begun to gather with unnatural speed. The air around them crackled, charged with an energy that made his skin prickle.

It was as if the very world had started to hold its breath.

"Do you feel it?" she asked, her voice low, almost a whisper.

Kael didn't need to answer. The unease had settled in his bones the moment the ruins had collapsed behind them. The earth, the wind, the flames—everything had seemed to shift, as though the world itself was realigning in response to something neither of them could yet see.

"I don't like it," Kael said finally, his voice rough. He turned away, pacing a few steps, trying to push the weight of the air off his chest. "Who was that man?"

Selene didn't turn to face him. Instead, she watched the clouds, her expression unreadable. "A messenger. Or perhaps a harbinger."

"A what?" Kael stopped, his brow furrowing. "A harbinger of what?"

Selene's shoulders tensed. "The storm."

The wind whistled between them, cold and sharp. Kael watched her for a moment longer before his gaze drifted back to the remains of the temple. Something about the way she said it— the storm—felt like a warning, but also a promise. A truth too heavy to speak outright.

He shifted on his feet, his fingers curling around the hilt of his sword. "And you think this… storm, whatever it is, is coming for us?"

She finally looked at him, her eyes narrowed in thought, a storm of her own swirling beneath her gaze. "Not just for us," she said softly. "For everyone."

The words hit him harder than he expected. The weight of her implication, the gravity of what she was saying—it all coiled in his chest like a snake preparing to strike. This wasn't just about her or him. This was something far bigger.

Kael took a breath, forcing the tension from his body. "Then we need to move."

Her gaze lingered on him for a moment, something flickering in her eyes. "Do you trust me?"

He blinked, taken off guard by the question. His gaze narrowed, his grip on his sword tightening. Trust. He had learned a long time ago that trust was a commodity few could afford. It was an illusion, a dangerous thing to give.

But there was something in her voice, a raw edge to her words that made him pause.

"I don't know," he said, the honesty of the statement a bitter pill in his mouth. "But I don't have a choice."

For a moment, neither of them moved. The air between them seemed to thicken, charged with unspoken understanding. Kael could feel it in the pit of his stomach—the tension, the pull between them that had been growing since they first met.

It wasn't just about survival anymore.

The silence stretched, then snapped as Selene turned sharply and began walking toward the forest that lay beyond the temple ruins. The storm, thickening in the distance, pushed her forward, as if it were guiding her. She moved with a quiet urgency, the kind that only came with knowledge of something terrible, something inevitable.

Kael followed without hesitation, every step he took an echo of the growing unrest in his chest.

They didn't speak as they moved through the forest, the only sound the soft rustle of leaves and the distant rumble of thunder. Kael couldn't help but watch her as she walked ahead of him, the way the light from the setting sun caught the curves of her figure, the soft sway of her hair with each step. She was both ethereal and grounded, the air around her alive with something he couldn't quite name.

For a moment, he forgot why he was following her. Forgot the storm. Forgot the messengers and the prophecy. All he could think of was her.

Her voice broke through his thoughts. "We're almost there."

Kael blinked, focusing again. They had reached a small clearing in the forest. In the center stood a stone archway, half-buried in the earth, weathered with age and neglect. The remnants of an old path, now overtaken by the wild, led to the structure.

Selene stopped at the entrance, her fingers brushing against the cool stone. Her eyes closed for a moment, and Kael could feel the shift in her energy, as though she were drawing something from the very air around them. The wind stirred, responding to her, a soft sigh that tugged at the corners of his mind.

"The Emberstone," she said, her voice barely audible. "This is where it all began."

Kael stepped closer, narrowing his gaze. "What is the Emberstone?"

Selene turned to him, her expression unreadable. "It's the heart of the balance. The last remnant of the ancient magic. The source of everything."

"And you think it's here?"

She nodded. "I know it is."

Kael stared at the archway, uncertainty gnawing at him. This wasn't just some hidden relic—it was something more. Something far more dangerous.

The wind began to pick up again, a sudden gust that made the trees around them sway. It was the kind of wind that made the hairs on the back of his neck stand on end, the kind that carried more than just the scent of the earth. It carried power. Magic.

Selene stepped forward, but as her foot touched the earth beneath the arch, the ground trembled.

The shift was subtle at first. The earth quivered like a breath being held too long. Then—

The Ruins of Fire and Sky

A low hum.

Kael's heart skipped a beat.

"Get back!" he shouted, grabbing her arm, pulling her away from the archway. But she resisted, her gaze locked on the stone.

"No," she said, her voice firm. "We need to see this through."

The hum grew louder, more insistent, vibrating through the ground beneath their feet. The trees around them groaned, as if protesting the disturbance. Kael's grip tightened on her wrist.

"Selene—"

She yanked her arm from his grasp, her eyes fierce. "I said no."

Before he could respond, the sky above them darkened, and a flash of lightning cracked through the air. The wind howled, bending the trees back as if the forest itself were being torn apart.

Kael's pulse raced. Something was happening—something beyond their control.

Selene closed her eyes, her face pale, as if she were drawing on something deep inside herself. "It's coming," she whispered.

"The storm?" Kael's voice was tight, barely above a whisper.

She didn't answer.

The hum from the ground grew to a deafening roar. The air around them sparked with static, and suddenly, the sky above them split open with a ferocity Kael had never seen before. The storm—no, it was more than a storm—was not just a force of nature. It was a force of magic.

And it was coming for them.

"Move!" Kael shouted.

But Selene didn't move.

Her eyes locked onto the storm, and for the briefest moment, Kael saw something in her eyes—something he couldn't place. It wasn't fear. It was acceptance.

She was ready.

Kael didn't have time to question it. He reached for her again, but before his fingers could make contact, the ground beneath them split open.

The world collapsed around them.

Five

A Debt to the Dark

The world felt as if it were breaking apart.

Kael's heart hammered in his chest as the ground trembled beneath his feet. The storm above them raged with an intensity he had never witnessed—black clouds swirling like a living thing, lightning flashing across the sky with a viciousness that sent tremors through the air.

But it wasn't the storm that had his attention.

It was Selene.

She stood at the center of the ruin, her arms stretched wide as if reaching for something only she could see. Her eyes were closed, her face pale, her expression one of focus, of determination. The wind whipped around her, tugging at her hair, pulling at the edges of her cloak. Magic—the kind that Kael had only heard of in legends—was crackling through the air like a living thing.

He should have pulled her away. He should have dragged her out of this ruin and back to safety.

But he couldn't.

Every instinct told him to run, to escape the forces at play here. And yet, he couldn't bring himself to move. She was doing something—something dangerous, but necessary. He could see it in the tension in her body, in the way she was rooted to the earth beneath her.

The storm was no longer just a force of nature. It was alive with power, alive with a purpose that neither of them fully understood.

"Selene!" Kael shouted, his voice cutting through the storm's fury. "What the hell are you doing?"

Her eyes snapped open, locking with his. The intensity in them nearly took his breath away. There was something in her gaze—something fierce, something raw—that made him take a step back.

"I'm trying to stop it," she said, her voice barely audible over the howl of the wind.

"Stop what?" Kael's chest tightened, and he took another step forward. "You're not going to stop a storm like this. It's magic—old magic. Too powerful. You'll get us both killed."

But she didn't flinch, didn't step back. She only stood taller, her voice unwavering. "I have to do this."

She reached into the air, her fingers tracing unseen patterns as if she were weaving something invisible. The wind followed her movements, spiraling around her like a tethered creature. Kael's breath hitched, a knot of fear tightening in his chest. He'd known she was powerful, but this... this was beyond anything he had ever imagined.

"You don't understand," she said, her voice tinged with regret, yet full of resolve. "This is the only way. If I don't do this now, if I don't take control—"

She cut herself off, a shudder running through her body. Her eyes fluttered closed again, and Kael's heart skipped a beat as he saw the pain flicker across her face.

He couldn't just stand there and watch her unravel.

He stepped forward, closing the distance between them in three quick strides. "Selene!" he barked, his voice sharp, desperate.

But before he could reach her, a violent gust of wind flung him back, slamming him into the side of a pillar. The impact knocked the air from his lungs, but he fought to stay conscious, to stay focused. He pushed himself up, shaking the dizziness from his head, but the world around him had already changed.

The storm had intensified.

The wind howled louder, a deafening roar that rattled the very bones of the ruin. The ground was shaking again, and the stone beneath Kael's feet was cracking. He stumbled, but something caught his attention—something was shifting in the air around them.

It was magic.

Kael couldn't deny it any longer. The storm wasn't just a storm. It was a manifestation of the ancient magic Selene had spoken of, the magic she had only just begun to wield. It was wild and untamed, reaching out, hungry for something. But what?

Kael's instincts screamed at him to run. To take her and flee before it was too late.

But he couldn't move. Not while she was still standing there, caught in the center of it all.

He looked back at her.

Her face was contorted with concentration, her brow furrowed as she struggled to maintain control over the spiraling winds. But there was something else in her expression—something darker, something Kael hadn't seen before.

Pain.

She was losing control.

"No!" Kael shouted, his voice laced with panic. "Selene, stop!"

But she didn't hear him. She was too deep in it now, too far gone. The winds around her were becoming more erratic, tearing at the earth, ripping through the stone. And then, just when it seemed as though the world would tear itself apart, the storm's fury suddenly stopped.

It was a stillness so complete that Kael felt as though the very air had been sucked out of the world.

The wind died.

The thunder faded.

And for a moment, Kael stood there, frozen in the quiet. But the silence wasn't peaceful. It was a kind of waiting. Something was coming.

Selene stood motionless, her hands still raised, her body trembling with exhaustion. Kael could see the strain in her face, the tightness around her eyes as though every muscle was fighting against her. The rawness of it all cut through him.

He took a tentative step toward her. "Selene…"

She lowered her arms slowly, her breath ragged. Her gaze met his, and for the first time, there was something almost… fragile in her expression.

"We're not safe," she said, her voice barely a whisper. "None of us are."

Kael took another step closer. His chest tightened as he saw the lines of exhaustion etched deep into her face, the way her body seemed to tremble with the weight of what she had just done. He couldn't leave her like this.

He reached out to her, but she flinched, taking a step back. The air between them was charged, heavy with the tension of everything left unsaid.

"Why?" he asked, his voice rough. "Why are you doing this?"

Her eyes softened, just for a moment. Then she blinked, and the hardness returned. "Because I owe a debt," she said, her voice almost lost in the windless space between them.

Kael's heart stuttered in his chest. A debt?

"Who?" he demanded, his voice rising. "Who do you owe this debt to?"

But she didn't answer. She simply turned away from him, walking toward the edge of the ruin, her back straight, her movements almost mechanical. Kael followed her, but the gulf between them seemed to grow with every step.

"You don't understand," she said quietly. "I don't have a choice."

"Of course you have a choice," Kael snapped, frustration bubbling up inside him. "You're not bound to anyone. You're free."

"No!" Kael shouted, his voice laced with panic. "Selene, stop!"

But she didn't hear him. She was too deep in it now, too far gone. The winds around her were becoming more erratic, tearing at the earth, ripping through the stone. And then, just when it seemed as though the world would tear itself apart, the storm's fury suddenly stopped.

It was a stillness so complete that Kael felt as though the very air had been sucked out of the world.

The wind died.

The thunder faded.

And for a moment, Kael stood there, frozen in the quiet. But the silence wasn't peaceful. It was a kind of waiting. Something was coming.

Selene stood motionless, her hands still raised, her body trembling with exhaustion. Kael could see the strain in her face, the tightness around her eyes as though every muscle was fighting against her. The rawness of it all cut through him.

He took a tentative step toward her. "Selene…"

She lowered her arms slowly, her breath ragged. Her gaze met his, and for the first time, there was something almost… fragile in her expression.

"We're not safe," she said, her voice barely a whisper. "None of us are."

Kael took another step closer. His chest tightened as he saw the lines of exhaustion etched deep into her face, the way her body seemed to tremble with the weight of what she had just done. He couldn't leave her like this.

He reached out to her, but she flinched, taking a step back. The air between them was charged, heavy with the tension of everything left unsaid.

"Why?" he asked, his voice rough. "Why are you doing this?"

Her eyes softened, just for a moment. Then she blinked, and the hardness returned. "Because I owe a debt," she said, her voice almost lost in the windless space between them.

Kael's heart stuttered in his chest. A debt?

"Who?" he demanded, his voice rising. "Who do you owe this debt to?"

But she didn't answer. She simply turned away from him, walking toward the edge of the ruin, her back straight, her movements almost mechanical. Kael followed her, but the gulf between them seemed to grow with every step.

"You don't understand," she said quietly. "I don't have a choice."

"Of course you have a choice," Kael snapped, frustration bubbling up inside him. "You're not bound to anyone. You're free."

She shook her head, a small, bitter smile curling at her lips. "I'm not free, Kael. Not anymore."

Kael reached for her arm, but this time she didn't pull away. She turned slowly, her gaze meeting his. Her eyes were like storms, swirling with emotions that he couldn't quite decipher.

"You want to know who I owe this debt to?" she said softly. "I owe it to the very magic that's been ripped from this world. And I will do whatever it takes to bring it back."

Kael's breath caught in his throat as he met her gaze. There was something in her eyes—something that spoke of sacrifice. Something that told him she would give everything to see this through.

He didn't know whether to run or stay.

But as she looked at him, something twisted in his chest. The fierce, unyielding fire in her—he couldn't walk away from that.

He couldn't leave her.

And he didn't want to.

"I'll help you," he said quietly.

Her eyes flickered, a brief flash of something—hope, fear, maybe both. Then, her gaze softened, just a little. "Thank you," she whispered.

But even as she spoke the words, Kael felt the unease in his chest deepen. This debt she spoke of, this magic she sought to control—it wasn't just a matter of survival anymore. It was a promise. A promise that would change everything.

For better… or for worse.

Six

Hearts Against the Storm

The air had thickened, heavy with the weight of a thousand unspoken words. Kael stood at the edge of the ruined clearing, watching Selene. She had turned away from him again, her back to the horizon, her shoulders stiff with the weight of something he couldn't touch.

The storm was still there, though now it seemed to wait—restless, coiled in the air like a predator waiting for the right moment to strike. Selene had called it, summoned it from the depths of the earth with nothing more than the whisper of her will. But in the silence that followed, the storm seemed almost… hesitant. Like a force that was unsure of its purpose without a master to direct it.

And for a brief moment, Kael wondered if Selene was as much a prisoner of this magic as she claimed to be. If the storm, like the fire within him, could consume her—mind, body, and soul—if she wasn't careful.

But he couldn't look away.

He couldn't stop himself from wanting to understand her.

From wanting to reach into that storm of her heart, that fierce, guarded place where her secrets hid beneath layers of bravado and iron will. He had seen the cracks in her resolve when she spoke of her debt, and they terrified him, even as they pulled him closer.

The fire and the wind—he had never believed in fate, in the pull of something greater than himself. But there was something about Selene that made him question everything he had ever known.

Something about her that made him feel like he was standing at the edge of a precipice, and if he moved just a little too far, he would fall.

Selene turned back to him, and for the first time, the mask she wore seemed to falter, just a fraction. Her eyes—stormy, filled with secrets—locked with his.

"I told you it's not a choice," she said, her voice barely above a whisper, as if the words themselves were too heavy to speak aloud.

Kael took a step toward her, his boots silent on the ground.

The wind was still swirling around them, a constant hum in the air. It should have been distracting, but instead, it seemed to emphasize the tension between them—the space that neither of them had yet bridged.

"I don't believe you," he said, his voice low, steady. "You always have a choice. You've had it your whole life."

Her lips tightened, but there was a flicker of something in her eyes, something softer than the stone-cold resolve she had worn for so long. "You don't know what it's like to carry this burden," she said quietly. "To be marked by something you can't control. To have your fate decided before you even knew it existed."

Kael swallowed, the weight of her words pressing against his chest. He didn't know, but he could guess. He had spent too many years watching people he cared about die because they couldn't escape the paths that had been carved out for them. The past never let go.

"I've been marked too," he said, his voice rough. "Not by magic, but by something else. Something I can't escape either."

Selene's gaze flickered over him, her expression softening, if only slightly. There was understanding there, a shared recognition of the burdens they both carried. But that moment of connection was fleeting, a breath caught in the wind before it was swept away.

The storm above them rumbled again, the distant thunder vibrating through the earth. Selene's face hardened, and she turned away from him once more, as though she couldn't bear to let him see her weakness.

"I don't need your pity," she said sharply, her voice cutting through the air like a blade. "I'm not some helpless child you can protect."

Kael's breath caught. The words struck him harder than he had expected. But it wasn't pity she was pushing away. It was something else. Something deeper.

Something that frightened her.

"Then stop pretending you can do this alone," Kael said, his voice harder now, more insistent. "I don't care about your past, or your debt, or whatever magic you think you're controlling. But if you think I'm just going to stand by and watch you destroy yourself—"

"I'm not destroying myself," she snapped, spinning around to face him, her eyes flashing with fire. "I'm saving what's left of this world. Don't you understand? This isn't about you, or me, or even the damned storm. This is about everything that's slipping through our fingers. Magic isn't just a weapon, Kael. It's the heart of everything. The balance of life itself."

He took a step toward her, feeling the pull between them like gravity. The wind swirled around them, as though the storm itself was listening to their words. Watching.

"You're right," he said softly. "It isn't just about us. But maybe…

maybe you don't have to bear that burden alone."

The words hung in the air between them, a fragile thing. Selene's gaze wavered, a flicker of doubt crossing her face. For a brief moment, she seemed on the verge of saying something—something that might change everything between them.

But then she closed her eyes, exhaling slowly as though to release the fragile moment. When she opened her eyes again, the hardness was back.

"I don't need anyone to save me, Kael," she said quietly, her voice filled with an exhaustion that was almost palpable. "Not even you."

Kael's chest tightened, and for a moment, he didn't know how to respond. He had never been good at letting people in. And yet, with her, it felt like something he couldn't hold back, no matter how hard he tried.

"Fine," he said, his voice rough with a mixture of frustration and something darker, something deeper. "But don't think for a second that I'm just going to walk away."

Selene's eyes flickered toward him, something unreadable in her expression. Then she turned back to the horizon, to the storm gathering above them, its fury still rippling through the air.

"I don't want you to walk away," she whispered, more to herself than to him.

Kael didn't speak. He could feel the weight of her words, feel the unspoken truth in them, and for the first time in days, something warm unfurled inside him.

But he didn't move closer. Not yet. Not when the distance between them still felt like an ocean.

The wind shifted again, and Selene's gaze locked onto the storm. Her face hardened. "We can't stay here. They'll come for us."

"They already have," Kael said grimly. "That man... the one who sent the storm. The Silver Order."

Selene's eyes darkened, and she looked away from him, her jaw tightening. "I know. But this... this isn't just about them anymore. They're just a symptom. The storm, the magic—it's all connected. And it's going to keep coming until we stop it."

Kael's chest tightened, a knot of unease settling in his stomach. "Stop it? How?"

Selene's eyes met his, and for the briefest moment, something like vulnerability flickered in her gaze. But it was gone as quickly as it came, replaced by a determination so fierce, it nearly took Kael's breath away.

"We find the Emberstone," she said quietly. "And we find a way to make the magic work again. For good. Or this world will fall apart."

Kael nodded, the weight of her words settling over him. There was no turning back now. He knew that, just as he knew that whatever was coming, whatever magic was stirring in the air, it wasn't something they could face alone.

He took a step closer to her, his voice low, steady. "Then we'll do it together."

She didn't answer at first. But when she finally spoke, her voice was softer, almost hesitant. "Together," she repeated.

And in that single word, Kael felt something shift between them. Something both fragile and irrevocable.

The storm was coming. And so was the magic.

But for the first time in a long while, Kael didn't feel entirely alone.

Seven

The Betrayer's Embrace

The night had descended like a cloak, heavy with the weight of the storm that still churned in the sky. Kael could feel the dampness in the air, the thick scent of earth and rain mingling with the faint, acrid sting of magic that lingered just below the surface. It was as though the world itself had become a tinderbox, the slightest spark away from igniting.

He wasn't sure how long they had been traveling, but the fatigue was starting to settle into his bones, weighing him down like a shadow that refused to leave. His eyes flickered to Selene, walking just ahead of him. Her stride was steady, purposeful, but Kael could see the weariness in the way her shoulders hunched, the tension in her jaw. She wasn't showing it, but he knew her better than that.

She had always been driven, but tonight there was something

different in her. The storm they had barely escaped was still pulling at her, like an unseen force just beyond her control. It wasn't just the magic, either. There was something in her eyes, something deeper that was driving her forward.

Kael's gaze lingered on her, his mind racing with questions he didn't dare ask. There was a debt, she had said. A debt that tied her to this mission, to the Emberstone. And the longer he traveled with her, the more he could feel the edges of that debt, the way it shaped her choices, her actions.

But tonight, it wasn't just the magic pulling at her. It was something else—something darker.

They had been walking for hours, through dense forests and across empty plains, and now, they found themselves at the edge of a small, abandoned village. The buildings were little more than broken shells, their walls cracked and crumbling, the windows shattered. The place had been abandoned long before the storm had started, and yet, it felt as though the world had paused here, waiting for something.

Selene stopped at the village's edge, her eyes scanning the ruins as though she were searching for something—or someone.

Kael stepped up beside her, his boots crunching on the gravel path. "What are we doing here?"

She didn't look at him at first. Instead, she moved forward, her steps sure and silent. "We're not alone," she said softly.

Kael's pulse quickened, his hand instinctively going to the hilt of his sword. "Who else knows we're here?"

"I don't know," she replied, her voice tight with the same unease that was beginning to crawl under Kael's skin. "But we'll find out soon enough."

They moved deeper into the village, the buildings casting long shadows in the flickering light of the moon. The air had thickened with the scent of damp stone and rotting wood, but beneath it all, there was something more. A faint trace of magic—dark and twisted, like a knife in the dark.

Kael's eyes narrowed, scanning the shadows. His instincts were on high alert, every fiber of his being telling him that danger was near. He hadn't felt this vulnerable in years, and it wasn't just because of the magic surrounding them. It was the sense that they were being watched—that someone, or something, was waiting for them to make a move.

"Stay close," he muttered, his voice low. Selene didn't answer, but her posture stiffened, and she nodded ever so slightly.

They moved through the village like ghosts, quiet and quick, their every step calculated. As they reached the center of the village, Kael's eyes fell on the small building at the far end—its roof caved in, the door ajar. There was something about it that felt... wrong.

"This is it," Selene said, her voice barely a whisper. She didn't need to say more. Kael could feel it, too. Whatever they were

The Betrayer's Embrace

searching for was inside.

He stepped forward, his hand on the hilt of his sword, but before he could reach the door, a voice rang out from the shadows.

"You shouldn't have come here."

Kael spun around, his hand instinctively going to his sword. Selene's eyes widened, but she didn't speak.

From the darkness stepped a man, his face hidden beneath a hood. He was tall, his posture straight and unyielding, but there was something about him that set Kael's nerves on edge. A familiarity, a recognition that he couldn't quite place.

The man's voice was smooth, almost mocking. "Did you really think you could just walk in and take what you wanted?"

Kael's grip tightened on his sword, but Selene stepped in front of him before he could draw it. She stood there, her gaze locked on the stranger, her expression unreadable.

"I knew you'd be waiting," she said, her voice steady despite the storm that swirled in the air around them.

The man tilted his head, as if surprised. "You knew?" His lips curled into a dark smile. "You always did have a way of seeing things before they happened. But you were never good at seeing who was behind them."

Kael's heart stuttered, recognition finally dawning. The man's voice, his presence—it was all too familiar.

"Varian?" Selene's voice was a mix of disbelief and anger.

The man's smile widened. "You remember me, then. How quaint."

Kael's mind raced, trying to place the name. Varian. The name echoed in his mind, a whisper of something long buried. This was no stranger. This was someone from Selene's past. Someone important.

"What do you want?" Selene asked, her voice cold, but Kael could see the subtle tremor in her hands, the way her posture had shifted just slightly. She was still the same, but there was a part of her that was cracking under the weight of this confrontation.

Varian's smile faded, replaced with something darker. "What I want is simple. The Emberstone. You've been searching for it, haven't you? You've come so far, only to find that it's already in the hands of those who have no intention of letting you take it."

Kael's mind clicked into place. The Silver Order. The connection between them. Varian wasn't just some mercenary or rogue. He was a member of the very group Selene had warned him about. The ones who had been erasing magic from the world.

And now, they had come for her.

The Betrayer's Embrace

Kael stepped forward, his voice low and menacing. "You're working for them?"

Varian's eyes flickered to Kael, his gaze assessing, calculating. "Working for them? No. I'm working for something much older, much more powerful than any of you could understand. You think you're in control of the magic, Selene, but you're just a pawn in a game far beyond your reach."

Selene's jaw tightened, but she didn't back down. "You're wrong."

Varian laughed, a low, throaty sound that sent a chill through Kael's spine. "Am I?"

Before Kael could react, the air shifted. A chill swept through the village, and for a moment, everything seemed to freeze. Then, without warning, Varian moved—fast, too fast. He raised a hand, and Kael felt the pressure of magic in the air, a suffocating weight that made it hard to breathe.

The ground beneath them cracked.

"Selene, get back!" Kael shouted, reaching for her, but it was too late.

Varian's magic slammed into them, sending both Kael and Selene sprawling across the ground. Kael gritted his teeth, fighting the crushing force that pressed against him, but he couldn't move, couldn't reach her.

Through the haze of magic and fear, Kael saw Selene struggling to rise, her hands shaking, her face twisted in concentration. She wasn't going to give in to him—not now.

"Selene!" Kael gasped, his voice hoarse.

And then, as if summoned by her will alone, the wind responded.

A gust of air surged forward, a blinding force that ripped through the village, shattering the spell that held them. For a moment, the world was filled with chaos—whispers of magic, the roar of the storm, the shattering of stone and wood.

And then, everything went silent.

Selene stood, her body trembling, but her eyes were fierce. The wind settled around her like an extension of her own will.

Varian's smile was gone now, replaced with a deep scowl. "You're not the only one who can control the elements, Selene."

Selene's voice was cold, unwavering. "Then let's see how well you control the storm."

Eight

The Silver Sky Fractures

The wind was a living thing, howling through the abandoned village like a beast on the hunt. It was relentless, tearing at the old stone and the broken timber, sending dust and debris spiraling into the air. Kael's body was heavy with exhaustion, but the pulse of magic crackling around them kept his senses sharp. The storm had returned—twisting, bending, spiraling into something darker, more dangerous. It wasn't just the wind that howled anymore. It was a presence, as if the world itself had split open, and something ancient, something terrible, had begun to claw its way back.

Selene stood at the center of the chaos, her body trembling from the effort of controlling the tempest she had unleashed. Her hair was whipped around her face, her eyes glowing with a fierce light, but there was something more in her gaze—something

Kael couldn't quite place. Fear, yes, but also something else. Desperation.

She had pushed herself too far.

Kael's instincts screamed at him to reach her, to pull her back from the edge of whatever abyss she was teetering on. But the air between them crackled with magic, and he knew—no matter how badly he wanted to help—he could do nothing to control the storm.

Not like she could.

"Selene!" His voice was drowned out by the fury of the winds, but he saw her head snap toward him. Her gaze was wild, as though she hadn't heard him at first. When their eyes met, he felt a shock of something he couldn't name. The storm seemed to pause for a moment, the air thick with a tension that had nothing to do with the weather. Everything around them stilled—just for a second.

Then, with a sharp cry, Selene's body arched forward, her arms outstretched as though she were trying to gather the very storm in her hands. Her breath came in ragged gasps, her fingers trembling with the weight of the magic she was wielding. The wind whipped around her like a torrent of wrath, pulling at her clothes, her hair, as though it meant to consume her whole.

Kael's heart clenched. He couldn't watch this.

Before he could move, Varian's voice rang out, calm and cutting through the chaos like a blade.

"You're too late, Selene."

The words sent a chill through Kael's spine. He turned sharply to see Varian standing just beyond the edge of the storm's reach, his eyes gleaming with an unsettling confidence. The wind didn't touch him. The air around him seemed to part, as though he was immune to the forces he had just unleashed.

Varian took a slow step forward, his gaze never leaving Selene. "You think you can control it?" he asked, his voice a low murmur. "You think this is still yours to command?"

Selene's head snapped up, her eyes blazing with a fury that burned brighter than the storm. She took a deep, shuddering breath and stood taller, gathering what remained of her strength. The winds flared up again, crashing around her in a violent frenzy. But this time, she didn't flinch.

"No," she said, her voice firm, cutting through the din of the storm. "This is mine. It always has been."

Varian's smile flickered, dark and knowing. "You're wrong. It never was." He took another step, his voice low and insistent. "You can't fight it, Selene. You never could. The wind, the fire—your magic—it was never meant to be yours. It was a gift, a curse, given to you by the very ones who controlled it long before you were born."

Kael's pulse quickened as he looked between them. The tension in the air was palpable, thick with unspoken history. Selene's eyes flashed with something that made Kael's stomach tighten.

"Who are you?" she demanded, her voice fierce but tinged with the faintest tremor. "What do you want from me?"

Varian's gaze softened slightly, as though pitying her. "You really don't know, do you?" He took another step forward, his eyes narrowing. "I should have known you'd be this ignorant. You've been used, Selene. All along."

The words hit her like a physical blow. Kael saw her flinch, her body stiffening under the weight of the accusation. She opened her mouth to speak, but the words seemed to fail her.

Kael moved forward, anger burning in his chest. "Enough, Varian," he spat. "We've heard your lies before. You're not fooling anyone."

Varian's eyes flicked to Kael, and for the first time, the man's smile faltered, just a little. "It's not lies, mercenary," he said, his tone colder now. "It's the truth. And you—" He waved a hand dismissively. "You have no place in this."

Kael's fingers tightened around the hilt of his sword, but before he could take another step, Selene's voice cut through the air, trembling with the weight of her words.

"No, Kael. He's right."

Kael's heart stopped. He looked at her, his gaze sharp with

disbelief. "What? What do you mean?"

Selene's eyes met his, her expression a mixture of sorrow and determination. "I've been trying to deny it. I've been trying to run from it. But the truth is…" She swallowed hard, her lips trembling. "The magic inside me—it's not just mine. It was given to me by someone I never understood. Someone who took everything from me."

Varian stepped closer, his eyes gleaming with satisfaction. "You see? The storm didn't just choose you, Selene. It was always meant for you. And the moment you found the Emberstone, the moment you truly unlocked the power inside you…" He trailed off, his gaze darkening. "That's when everything changed. And not for the better."

Kael's mind reeled, the words falling into place like pieces of a puzzle he wasn't sure he wanted to solve. He turned to Selene, his voice rough with a mixture of anger and fear. "What is he talking about, Selene? What is the Emberstone?"

She closed her eyes for a moment, as though steeling herself for the truth. Then, when she opened them again, there was a new light in her eyes—a sadness, but also a resolve that Kael hadn't seen before.

"The Emberstone is the heart of the world," she said softly, her voice carrying the weight of a truth too terrible to ignore. "It holds the power of all the elements, Kael. It's what kept the balance intact." She looked at Varian, her eyes narrowing. "And when the Silver Order destroyed it, when they fractured the balance…" She faltered for a moment, then continued, her voice barely above a whisper. "I was the one chosen to restore it."

The words hung in the air like a spell, heavy and suffocating. Kael's mind spun, his chest tight with the realization of what she was saying. The Emberstone. The balance of magic. Selene—she had always known, always carried this burden.

But what had it cost her?

Varian stepped forward, his voice smooth, like honey laced with poison. "And now you know the truth, Selene. You were never meant to restore anything. You were always meant to destroy it."

Kael's heart skipped. "What?"

Selene's gaze flickered to him, her expression a mixture of regret and something darker. "I didn't want this, Kael," she whispered. "But the magic, the storm—it won't stop until it's all gone."

Varian's eyes gleamed. "You understand now, don't you? You can't fight it. The storm isn't just a weapon. It's the end. And once it's begun, there's no going back."

Kael's hand clenched around his sword. He didn't care what Varian said. He didn't care about the storm or the Emberstone. He only cared about Selene—about the woman standing before him, broken and lost, yet still fighting.

"No," Kael said, his voice low but firm. "We're not done. We'll fight. We'll find a way to fix this."

Selene's eyes met his, her gaze filled with something unreadable. Then, just as quickly, the wind picked up again, tearing at them both, a sign of the magic that still gripped her, still controlled her.

She stepped back, her voice trembling. "You can't save me, Kael. The storm is already here."

And with those words, the silver sky above them fractured, splitting open like glass, and Kael knew, with a sickening certainty, that nothing would ever be the same.

Nine

The Fire Within

The wind howled around them, a tempest that seemed to echo the chaos within Kael's chest. His breath came in short, ragged bursts as he stood at the edge of the broken village, watching Selene. She was a silhouette against the storm—tall, defiant, as if she could stand against the very forces that threatened to consume everything. But Kael could see it in the way her shoulders trembled, the faint flicker of vulnerability in her eyes every time she looked away from him.

This wasn't just about the Emberstone anymore. This wasn't just about the magic that had been ripped from the world. It was about her. And no matter how much he told himself to stay focused, to keep his emotions in check, he knew that it was already too late.

She had said it herself. The storm wasn't just a force. It was a harbinger. And now, standing in the ruins of the village, Kael could feel it closing in. The air itself seemed to hum with it, a tremor in the earth beneath his feet that spoke of something darker—a reckoning.

"Selene..." Kael's voice was barely audible above the rising wind, but she heard him. Her head turned slowly, her eyes searching his face as if trying to find something in him that had long since vanished.

"I didn't want you to see this," she said, her voice strained, raw. The words stung more than Kael expected. She wasn't just pushing him away. She was pushing herself away. From everything.

Kael took a step forward, ignoring the wind that tried to force him back. His hand reached out, fingers brushing against the bare skin of her arm. The contact was like fire and ice, sending a shock through both of them. She didn't pull away, but he could feel the distance, like an invisible barrier that she was desperately trying to keep between them.

"I'm not afraid of the storm, Selene," he said, his voice rough with frustration. "I'm afraid of losing you."

Her eyes flickered, something shifting behind them—an emotion she refused to show, one she couldn't hide no matter how hard she tried. The vulnerability in her gaze made his heart ache. It was something too raw, too honest for the woman who had always masked her emotions with fire and wind.

"You should be afraid, Kael," she whispered, the words almost lost to the wind. "I've already lost myself. What makes you think I can be the person you think I am?"

Kael's chest tightened. The words cut deeper than any sword could. She was telling him she wasn't who he thought she was—and maybe she wasn't. Maybe the woman standing before him wasn't the same woman he had trusted, the woman who had fought beside him.

But as much as she pushed him away, Kael knew this was a battle he couldn't walk away from. Not now. Not when everything they had fought for was on the verge of slipping through their fingers.

"I don't care who you think you are, Selene," he said, his voice steady despite the tremble in his chest. "I care about who you are."

The storm raged louder around them, but in that moment, everything else seemed to fall away. The magic in the air, the crackling tension that threatened to tear them apart—it all felt distant. All that remained was her, standing before him, her expression conflicted, torn between the desire to give in and the need to protect herself.

For a long moment, she said nothing. Then, with a slow, deliberate movement, she pulled away from him.

"I can't," she said, her voice breaking. "I can't let you in. I can't risk you."

Kael's heart clenched, his fists balling at his sides. "You don't get to decide that," he said, his voice a mixture of pain and anger. "I'm already in. Whether you want me here or not, I'm not leaving you to face this alone."

Her eyes darkened, a shadow crossing her face. "You don't understand, Kael. The magic—it's too much. It'll burn us both. I won't let you be consumed by it."

His eyes hardened. "Then stop running from it. Stop running from me. We can do this together."

For a brief moment, her gaze softened, a flicker of hope in her eyes before it vanished. She turned away from him again, her hand reaching up to pull the winds closer. Her voice was quiet, but the desperation in it hit him like a hammer.

"I'm not who you think I am," she whispered. "I can't be."

And in that moment, Kael understood. She wasn't just trying to protect him from the storm. She was trying to protect him from herself. From the force that lay within her, the magic that had once been a gift but now felt like a curse.

It was a curse that threatened to tear them apart.

Kael reached for her again, his hand gripping her wrist this time, stopping her before she could retreat into herself again.

"Don't run from this, Selene. You're not alone."

Her eyes locked with his, the storm between them like a living thing, crackling with magic and emotion. For a moment, neither of them moved. Then, slowly, she nodded, her shoulders sagging with the weight of something unspoken.

"I don't want to hurt you," she whispered.

Kael's grip on her wrist softened, but he didn't let go. "You won't. Not if we face this together."

The wind around them shifted, almost as though it were listening to their words, responding to the pull between them. Kael could feel the magic swirling in the air, could taste it on his tongue—a promise, a danger, and a temptation all wrapped into one.

And then it happened.

The storm seemed to pull in on itself, contracting, the air thickening with the hum of ancient power. The ground trembled beneath their feet, and Kael could feel the magic inside Selene, surging to the surface like fire threatening to escape a cage. The winds roared louder, the air became charged with a deadly force, and for a heartbeat, Kael thought it might all come crashing down on them.

And then it stopped.

The silence that followed was deafening. For a moment, Kael didn't dare to breathe. He felt her pulse beneath his fingertips, the thrum of her heartbeat faster than usual, but steady.

And then, slowly, the storm began to settle. The winds calmed, the magic receded, and everything around them stilled. But in the aftermath of the storm, Kael could feel something shifting between them. Something had broken, but it was a fracture that might heal.

Selene's hand was still in his, and for the first time, she didn't pull away. She met his gaze, her eyes filled with something he couldn't name. It was fear, yes, but it was also something else. Something more vulnerable than he had ever seen before.

"Kael..." Her voice was barely above a whisper, but the rawness of it cut through him. "I don't know if I can control it anymore. The magic, the storm—it's not just something I carry. It's a part of me."

Kael took a deep breath, his hand tightening around hers. "Then we'll face it together. I don't care how strong it is. I don't care how dangerous it is. As long as I'm with you, we'll find a way."

For a moment, she didn't answer. But then, just as he thought she might pull away again, she stepped closer, her forehead resting lightly against his chest. The gesture was small, but it spoke volumes. She was allowing him in, just a little, just enough to see the cracks in her armor.

"Together," she whispered, the word barely audible above the stillness of the world around them.

Kael closed his eyes for a moment, feeling the weight of everything they were about to face. But with her here, with her trust in him, he knew—whatever came next, they would face it together.

And no storm could take that from them.

Ten

Love and Ruin

The world was quieter now.

It wasn't that the storm had subsided entirely, nor had the magic in the air faded. The wind still stirred with a kind of quiet violence, and the hum of ancient power lingered just beneath the surface, pressing against Kael's skin like the weight of something too big, too dangerous, to ignore. No, it wasn't the quiet that unsettled him—it was the stillness. The moment after the storm, when everything seemed to hang in balance, uncertain of what would come next.

Selene stood just beyond him, her figure outlined by the faint light of the silver moon, which shone through the gaps in the clouds. The storm had passed, but the tension between them—between all that had been said, all that had been left unsaid—still lingered in the air.

Kael could feel her, even from a distance, the pull between them like the irresistible force of a tide that couldn't be stopped. It had always been there, since the first moment their paths had crossed, but now, with the storm receding, the storm within her—within them—seemed to pulse with an intensity that threatened to break them both. He could still taste the magic in the air, the power that Selene had unleashed, the same power that had burned through her and left her standing on the precipice of something too dangerous to name.

"Kael…" Selene's voice broke through the silence, soft but heavy, her tone a mixture of something akin to fear and longing. She wasn't looking at him yet, and for a moment, he wasn't sure if she even wanted to.

He didn't know if he could bear the weight of her words, the weight of everything they had just faced. But even as he stood there, watching her, he knew one thing with absolute certainty: she needed him. Maybe more than she was willing to admit. And maybe, just maybe, he needed her too.

He took a step closer, his boots crunching softly on the damp earth. The air was thick with the scent of wet soil, of something more primal—the aftertaste of the magic that still lingered, woven into the very fabric of the world around them. He could feel it in his chest, beating in time with his heart. It wasn't just the storm. It was everything. Everything that was about to break loose.

"I don't know what's happening inside me," Selene whispered, her voice barely audible over the rustle of the wind. "I can feel it, Kael. The storm. The magic. It's growing stronger, and it's..." She trailed off, her words faltering. He could hear the fear in her voice, the fear that she couldn't control what she had become.

"You're not alone," Kael said, his voice steady, even though his own pulse raced with a mixture of confusion and something darker, something deeper. "You've never been alone in this. Not with me."

She didn't look at him. Not yet. But he saw the way her shoulders tensed, the slight way her hands fisted at her sides, as if she were trying to hold something back. "You don't understand," she said, her voice shaking now. "The power—it's not just mine. It's connected to everything. To the balance of the world. To the Emberstone. And the moment I unleashed it, I... I lost myself in it. I don't even know if I can find my way back."

Kael's chest tightened. He stepped closer, reaching for her, though he wasn't sure if it was his heart or his instincts pulling him forward. "You don't have to find your way back alone. Let me help you, Selene. Whatever it is that you're running from inside yourself, we can face it together."

For a long moment, she stood there, her back to him, her breath shallow, as if she were trying to gather the strength to face whatever it was that had been haunting her.

And then, slowly, she turned to face him.

Her eyes were stormy, filled with something fierce, something desperate. But in that fierceness, Kael saw the cracks—the vulnerability she kept buried deep inside.

Her voice was barely a whisper. "I don't know how to let go of it, Kael. It's too much. It's always been too much."

Her words stung, but there was something in them—a rawness—that made his heart ache for her. He had seen the fire in her, the strength that kept her standing when everything around her was falling apart. But now, in the wake of the storm, he saw something else. He saw a woman torn between the power she wielded and the fear of losing herself to it.

Kael reached for her hand, his fingers brushing the skin of her wrist. "You don't have to let go of anything," he said softly. "Just let me help you hold it. Just for a little while."

For a moment, she didn't move. But then, slowly, she met his gaze, and for the first time in what felt like forever, she let herself believe him. She let herself believe that she wasn't alone in this.

And then, without warning, she pulled him to her.

Her lips crashed against his, desperate, hungry, as though the storm between them had finally broken, and there was nothing left but the raw need to be close. To be together. The kiss was all fire and magic, as if the very world had shifted, and for the briefest moment, the storm inside them both quieted. It was everything Kael had longed for since the first moment he had laid eyes on her—the connection, the intensity, the pull that neither of them could fight.

But it wasn't just passion. It was a promise. A silent vow, made in the depths of the storm, that no matter what came next, they would face it together.

When she finally pulled away, her breath was shallow, her forehead resting against his. Her voice was hoarse, her words tinged with something between relief and fear. "I'm not who you think I am, Kael. The magic—it's too dangerous. And I—"

Kael stopped her before she could continue. He cupped her face in his hands, forcing her to look at him, to see the truth in his eyes. "You're the woman I've come to trust, Selene. Not the magic. Not the storm. Just you. And I'm not leaving you."

She trembled against him, her body betraying the strength she tried so hard to keep hidden. The storm inside her still raged, but she wasn't alone anymore. Not in this. Not with him.

"I can't do this alone," she whispered, her voice breaking, the words falling like a confession she had never allowed herself to speak. "I'm scared, Kael. I'm scared of what I might become."

Kael's heart clenched. The fear in her voice, the rawness of it—it cut through him like a blade. "You won't become anything you don't want to, Selene. You're stronger than you think. I've seen it."

Her eyes searched his, as if looking for something. Something that would prove he wasn't just saying the words. "You don't know what this magic can do. What it's done to me. I've lost so much already. I'm not sure I can stop it."

Kael's fingers brushed against her cheek, his touch gentle, despite the fire that still burned between them. "We'll stop it. Together."

The wind shifted again, this time more gently. It didn't rage anymore. It moved with purpose, as if it had heard their words. And in the stillness that followed, the world seemed to hold its breath, waiting for something to change. For something to give.

Selene closed her eyes, her body relaxing slightly against his. For the first time in what felt like forever, Kael saw her as she truly was—not just the warrior, the force of nature, but the woman behind it all. And in that moment, he knew that no matter what came next, no matter how dangerous the storm became, he would be there.

Because she wasn't alone.

And neither was he.

Eleven

The Final Ember

The world was darker than it had ever been. The storm had finally subsided, but the weight of the night hung heavily in the air, as if the earth itself was holding its breath. The remnants of the tempest still whispered in the trees, a low hum of magic that refused to die. Kael stood at the edge of the clearing, his gaze fixed on Selene. She was standing alone in the center, her figure bathed in the eerie light of the dying fire. The flames danced, casting flickering shadows across her face, but it wasn't just the fire that illuminated her. There was something else now—something in her eyes, a spark that hadn't been there before.

For the first time, Kael could see her clearly. Not just the warrior, the woman of strength and defiance, but the person underneath it all. The one who was struggling, who was afraid of what the magic inside her might turn her into. He could feel the heat of it in the air, even now. But something had changed. She had changed.

She turned toward him, her expression unreadable. "You've seen it, haven't you?" Her voice was quiet, almost hesitant, but the weight of her words hit him like a physical blow. "The power. The storm inside me."

Kael's heart tightened in his chest. He could feel the truth of it in every fiber of his being. He had seen it, felt it—the way the storm surged in her, a part of her that she couldn't escape. But it wasn't just the power that had changed her. It was the way she had started to accept it, to acknowledge it.

"I've seen more than the storm," Kael said, his voice steady despite the chaos swirling around them. "I've seen you. All of you."

Her eyes flickered, and for a moment, he thought she might look away. But she didn't. She held his gaze, as though searching for something in him that she couldn't quite find.

"I'm scared, Kael," she whispered. "Scared of what I might become." Her voice was raw, stripped of the strength she usually wore like armor. "The magic—it's not just something inside me anymore. It's a part of everything. A part of the world. And if I lose control, if I—"

Kael stepped forward, closing the distance between them, and took her hand in his. "You won't lose control," he said firmly. "You're not alone in this."

She looked at him, her eyes filled with something darker now—something that resembled despair. "But I've already lost myself," she said. "The magic, the Emberstone, it's all connected. It was never meant for someone like me."

The words struck him like a blade. He could see the pain in her face, the anguish she had tried to bury for so long. But it was there now, written in every line of her expression. She was still fighting, still searching for a way out.

"I don't care what you think you've lost," Kael said, his voice soft but firm. "You're not alone in this, Selene. You never will be." He squeezed her hand, feeling the warmth of her skin against his. "Whatever this magic is, we'll face it together. No matter what happens."

Her gaze softened, just a little, and Kael saw the faintest flicker of something—something close to hope. But it was fleeting. She turned away, her gaze drifting toward the horizon, where the first hints of dawn were breaking through the darkness. The storm might have passed, but something else was coming.

"I don't know if I can stop it," she said, her voice barely above a whisper.

Kael's chest tightened. He wanted to say something—anything—to make her believe that everything could still be fixed, that there was still a way to control the magic, to stop the storm before it consumed her. But the words wouldn't come. Instead, he reached out, pulling her gently into his arms. She didn't resist, and for a moment, everything was still—just the two of them, wrapped in the warmth of their shared breath, the firelight casting their shadows long across the ground.

"I'll be here," Kael whispered into her hair. "I'll always be here."

Selene's breath hitched, and for a moment, he thought she might pull away, but she didn't. She stayed in his arms, her body pressed against his as if she were seeking solace in his presence. And maybe she was. Because in this moment, there was no magic. No storm. Just the two of them, trying to make sense of everything that had led them here.

"I don't deserve this," she whispered, her voice thick with emotion. "I don't deserve you."

Kael pulled back slightly, lifting her chin so that she would look him in the eyes. "You don't have to deserve anything, Selene. You are everything to me."

Her eyes searched his face, as if trying to find the truth in his words. "I've hurt people. I've made mistakes. I've—"

Kael pressed a finger to her lips, silencing her. "We all have our pasts, Selene. But it's what we do now that matters." He took her face in his hands, his thumb brushing over her cheek. "You're not the mistakes you've made. You're the person standing right in front of me."

For a long moment, they simply stood there, the world around them growing quieter, the storm receding into the distance. But the tension in the air remained, a silent promise of what was to come. Whatever it was, Kael knew one thing for certain: he couldn't let her face it alone. And if that meant walking into the fire with her, then so be it.

"I can feel it," Selene said suddenly, her voice tight. "The magic. It's calling to me." Her breath hitched, and Kael could feel her pulse quickening beneath his fingertips. "It wants to consume me."

"No," Kael said firmly, shaking his head. "It doesn't. Not if we stand together. We're stronger than this, Selene. I believe in you."

She closed her eyes, as though trying to find some semblance of control within herself. The air around them began to shift again, the magic humming like a distant echo, pulling at her, testing her resolve. Kael could feel it too—the power that lay beneath the surface, the storm that still raged within her, but it wasn't just her. It was in him, too. In the way their fates had intertwined, in the way the storm had become as much a part of him as it was of her.

Kael kissed her then, gently but with an urgency that spoke of everything he couldn't say, everything he couldn't express in words. The magic crackled in the air around them, a reminder of the forces that threatened to tear them apart, but in that moment, it didn't matter. Nothing else mattered. Not the storm, not the Emberstone, not the choices they had yet to make. There was only the two of them, their hearts beating in sync, their souls entwined.

When the kiss finally broke, Selene's breath was ragged, her forehead pressed against his. Her eyes were closed, her body trembling with the force of emotions she had kept hidden for too long.

"I'm scared," she whispered, her voice thick with vulnerability. "Scared of what I might become."

Kael held her tighter, pulling her back to him. "You're not becoming anything you don't want to be," he said softly. "You're not alone. Not with me."

And for the first time, Selene let herself believe him. She let herself trust that, no matter what came next, they would face it together.

Twelve

The Silver Sky

The first rays of dawn broke through the blackened sky, casting an eerie light across the clearing. The storm had passed, but its weight still lingered in the air. Kael could feel it in the tremor beneath his feet, in the heavy stillness between every breath. The world was waiting, as though it had paused in anticipation of something—or someone—changing the very course of its path.

Selene stood a few paces ahead of him, her back to the rising sun, her face bathed in the soft glow of the new day. The wind had died down, but the magic still lingered in the air, like a living thing waiting to be called upon. Kael could feel it in the way his heart raced, the pull of something ancient stirring beneath the surface. And it wasn't just the power she wielded—it was the power that seemed to bind them both, drawing them together even as it threatened to tear them apart.

Her hands were clenched at her sides, her body stiff with the tension that had never truly left her. She had come so far, had faced so much, and yet the storm inside her had not fully subsided. There was something darker at the heart of it, something Kael could feel every time he looked at her—something that made him wonder if they had truly seen the worst of it yet.

"Selene..." he called her name, his voice breaking through the quiet of the dawn.

She didn't turn to him immediately, and in that moment, Kael felt the distance between them stretch wider, like the horizon before him—a gap he couldn't cross without her help. But then she did turn, her eyes meeting his with an unreadable expression.

"I'm afraid," she whispered, her voice thick with the weight of unshed tears. "Not just for myself, Kael. For all of us."

Kael took a step toward her, his boots crunching softly on the dry earth. The silence between them was deafening, the air still heavy with magic. The kind of magic that had once been a force for balance and now threatened to consume them all.

"Don't be," Kael said, his voice firm. "We're in this together. No matter what happens, I'm not leaving you. Not now. Not ever."

Her eyes softened just the slightest bit, but there was still a flicker of something behind them—a fear too deep to ignore. She swallowed hard, her throat working as if the words she needed to say were lodged there, unwilling to escape.

"I don't know how much longer I can keep this up," she said, her voice barely audible now. "The magic, the storm—it's inside me, Kael. It's part of me. And I don't know how to stop it."

Kael reached her side in three long strides, his hand resting gently on her arm. He could feel the heat of her skin even through the fabric of her sleeve, the pulse of life in her veins that matched the wildness in the air. There was something primal in it, something raw and untamed that threatened to break free.

"I'm not asking you to stop it," he said, his voice soft but determined. "I'm asking you to trust me. We'll find a way. Together."

Selene's eyes flickered toward the horizon, where the first light of the morning painted the sky in shades of silver and gold. The landscape, once so familiar, now felt like a different world entirely. A world on the brink of destruction. The storm that had ravaged the land was over, but the battle was far from won.

"You don't understand," she whispered, her voice cracking

as if the words themselves were a weight she could no longer carry. "I'm not just holding the magic inside me, Kael. I'm the key to restoring it. But I don't know if I can control it. Not anymore."

Kael's hand tightened on her arm, pulling her gently toward him. "You don't have to control it," he said, his voice filled with conviction. "You just have to be willing to let it work with you. Let it flow through you. Together, we can make this work."

For a long moment, she didn't respond. But then, slowly, she turned to face him, her eyes searching his, as if she were looking for something she couldn't find. She didn't say anything, but Kael could see the struggle within her, the storm that raged not just in the world around them, but inside her.

"I don't know if I can do this," she whispered, her voice thick with fear and uncertainty. "What if I lose myself? What if the storm takes over? What if I become something else?"

Kael lifted his hand to her face, his fingers brushing lightly against her cheek. The touch was gentle, grounding, and for the first time in a long while, Selene didn't pull away. She closed her eyes for a brief moment, as if letting herself sink into the comfort of his touch.

"You won't lose yourself," Kael said softly. "You've always been the one to control it. The magic might be inside you, but it doesn't define you. You define it."

Selene opened her eyes and looked at him, her expression softened but still filled with doubt. "But what if I can't hold on? What if the magic takes me over completely?"

Kael took a deep breath, feeling the weight of her words pressing against him. He could see the fear in her eyes, the vulnerability she had fought so hard to hide. He could feel it, too, deep in his chest, but he refused to let it overwhelm him.

He refused to let it tear them apart.

"You're stronger than you think," he said, his voice unwavering. "And I'll be here. Every step of the way. No matter what comes."

For a long time, they stood there in silence, the wind tugging at their clothes, the magic still humming faintly in the air. And then, without warning, Selene took a deep breath, her chest rising and falling with the weight of what she was about to do.

"I have to do this," she whispered, her voice filled with a quiet determination. "I have to make it right."

Kael stepped back, giving her the space she needed. He didn't say anything, but he didn't need to. He could see the resolve in her eyes, the fire that burned brighter than the storm itself.

Selene closed her eyes and extended her arms, the magic in the air swirling around her. Kael watched as she lifted her hands, drawing the wind to her, feeling the power building within her. The air crackled with energy, the storm swirling once more, but this time it wasn't wild. This time, it was controlled, as if she had finally learned to embrace it.

Kael held his breath as the magic surged around her, wild and beautiful and terrifying all at once. The wind howled as it gathered around her, the fire from the nearby camp flickering in response, feeding into the storm. It was like watching the birth of a new world, a world that could be shaped by their will—or destroyed by it.

For a moment, it seemed as though everything would collapse. The air was thick with power, the ground trembling beneath their feet. Kael felt the pressure in his chest, the weight of the world bearing down on them both.

But then, Selene's voice broke through the chaos, steady and sure.

"Now," she whispered. "We end this."

Kael felt the magic settle, the storm receding as she took control, shaping it, guiding it. The air hummed with energy, but it wasn't the same as before. It wasn't destructive. It was focused, directed. Selene was no longer running from the magic. She was embracing it.

The storm quieted, the winds dying down, the earth still beneath their feet. For the first time in what felt like forever, Kael felt a peace settle over them, the kind that came when two forces had finally come to terms with one another.

Selene turned to him, her eyes glowing with the aftermath of what they had just done. The storm had passed. But the magic was still alive, still a part of them.

Kael stepped toward her, his hand reaching for hers. "We did it," he said, his voice low but filled with awe.

Selene's lips curled into the faintest of smiles. "We did," she whispered. "Together."

And as the first light of dawn spread across the horizon, Kael knew that whatever came next, they would face it together. Because the storm was no longer something to fear—it was a part of them, a part of their world, and together, they would control it.

Together, they would change the world.

www.ingramcontent.com/pod-product-compliance
Lightning Source LLC
LaVergne TN
LVHW020429080526
838202LV00055B/5100